# SOLO SOUNDS

## FOR TRUMPET

**Piano Accompaniment-Levels 1-3**  **Volume 1**

D1317011

Cover Credit: Ace Music Center, North Miami, Florida
Yamaha International Corporation Musical Instrument Division

Editor: Jack Lamb

EL03340

# The Little House

Bobby Herriot and Howard Cable

# Up And Down And Round About

Bobby Herriot and
Howard Cable

(For Francesco di Blasi)

# "Nelda" Minuetto

Leonard B. Smith (ASCAP)

Copyright © 1973 by BELWIN MILLS PUBLISHING CORP.
15800 N.W. 48th Avenue, Miami, Florida 33014

(To Guido Fucinari)

# Valse "Au Printemps"

Leonard B. Smith (ASCAP)

# Rusty's Song

Bobby Herriot and
Howard Cable

# Prelude

Henry Johnson

A little faster (flowing)

# Scherzo

Edgar L. Barrow

# Country Dance

William Pelz

Moderato con moto

# Petite Valse

G.W. Lotzenhiser

# The Valiant

William Pelz

Moderato con moto

# Ballad In Blue
## (Tone Poem)

Robert Girlamo
*Edited by Major Herman Vincent*

# Russian Hymn

*Arranged by Major Herman Vincent*

# Caprice

Major Herman Vincent

# Trumpet Voluntary

Henry Purcell
*Arranged by Bobby Herriot*